MAKE MONEY FROM

BLOGGING

A PRACTICAL GUIDE TO START A SUCCESSFUL BLOG TODAY AND EARNING PASSIVE INCOME

TABLE OF CONTENTS

INTRODUCTION

I want to thank you and congratulate you for purchasing the book, "MAKE MONEY FROM BLOGGING – A PRACTICAL GUIDE TO START A SUCCESSFUL BLOG TODAY AND EARNING PASSIVE INCOME".

So you're seeking out information on how you can earn an income by writing blogs and promoting products through affiliate links, etc. You have made the right decision by purchasing this BOOK. To be truthful, making money through writing blogs is not as easy as just writing a blog and watching as the money comes rolling in.

If you haven't read much yet on the subject, you'll soon be confused by all the contradicting information. You can literally read a endless library of opposing viewpoints with respect to writing blogs. But like everything there are simple rules to follow.

Take the time to understand and verify the information you read. Trust me, after you've absorbed enough information in this BOOK and used it, you'll start to be able to filter out the good from the bad.

Making good money through blogging is possible. People do it every day. But it takes a lot of work. Do your work, stay the course and don't become discouraged and you can find financial freedom.

While I don't claim to be a top leading expert in this field, I do know enough and I care enough to hope that you get enough facts about the art of blogging and how to make money with your blog and the art of blogging for dollars.

In this book are embedded steps to get you started on your journey to creating a blog for profit. Follow this step-by-step guide that shows you how to be a blogger who provides value to your readers.

Thanks again for downloading this book, I hope you enjoy it!

CHAPTER 1

WHY SHOULD YOU START BLOGGING?

Before you even start to create your own blog to make money, it is necessary to know what a blog really is. The term blog is actually derived from the word Weblog or Web log. Back in the days, around the late 1990's, these Web logs were utilized by individuals to track updates and references to other resources online.

They served as journals, which made them useful as a publishing tool for the user's stream of consciousness. Of course, the readers can still comment and share their thoughts on just about anything under the sun.

Technically, blogs are also known as CMS or Content Management Systems. Being a CMS, blogs allow the writers to easily publish to a specific Web site and manage the content without the need of having to deal with the program code.

Publishing software also provides users with a GUI or Graphical User Interface for easy pointing and clicking of their articles.

Through the use of easy-to-do procedures, you can perform configurations and set up, which can ease your job as a blogger since the tool can automatically organize your published articles the next time you publish.

The main question is; why should you start blogging?

The first thing you need to know is that blogging can enhance and support your online communications. However, you must first understand the outcome of your blog that you desire in order to attain success. The main reason why you should start blogging is that it can be both an excellent outlet for your frustrations or excitement.

What you are passionate about and profitable at the same time. It does not mean that if you are not into blogging, you should not blog. Being in a business, especially those with dealings on the Internet, requires you to establish a clientele that are actually interested in your products or services.

More so, if you are handling a business, there is a good chance that your competition is blogging about products and services that they sell or provide. This is an easy method for you to examine your competition and analyse what the clients' preferences are.

Additionally, blogs can create strong customer relationships since your target market can easily and directly communicate with the authority within your business.

This kind of opportunity is hard to resist since a strong customer relationship can eventually lead to lasting trust to your product and services; hence, eventual increase in your revenue.

CHAPTER 2

STEP 1 - FIND A BLOG IDEA (BUSINESS IDEA) WHICH "FITS" YOU!

In order to determine how to start a blog, we've still got to go back to the basics, namely understanding and determining what is an excellent and profitable blog idea.

For most bloggers, especially those new to the blogosphere, coming up with ideas to write about on a regular basis can be a big challenge. We've all faced it at one time or another: the equivalent to traditional writers block, trying to figure out what to say stymies many and unfortunately leads most of us to abandoning our beloved blogs early and prematurely.

You've undoubtedly seen this through the countless blogs that have limited blog posts and/or lengthy gaps between blog articles. Surveys indicate that the first things people generally notice about blogs, before they read the first word of a post, are the number of blog entries and the date of the most recent post (# of comments rates equally high).

In the world of blogging, there is one thing we know for sure. If you are not blogging with any degree of regularity, rest assured your site visitors are more likely to click away faster than you can say "I'm a blogger".

For those of you who want to be known as a blogger, or simply as someone who wants to get more people to read what you have to say, developing a method for generating ideas for new content is the key to getting your blog read by more visitors. Fortunately, there are tons of great resources available to help you come up with great ideas without having to re-invent the wheel.

If you have a weblog, you probably already know the value of adding dynamic content to your site. From a search engine perspective, developing fresh content in the form of regular blog posts helps to generate more relevance and potentially get your website listed higher up in the search engine results pages (SERPs) for your desired niche.

In fact, unless you have an ecommerce site where products are continually changing, your blog becomes the most likely part of your website to change with any regularity. That's why it's so important to make sure you are always developing fresh ideas to incorporate into your blog.

So how do you efficiently generate new ideas for your blog?

Here are a few tips to help you get started.

Decide what you want to write about

If you have a weblog, you probably already know the answer to that question. Still, coming up with new ideas can prove difficult. The good news is you may have great content in waiting just with the things you experience in your daily routine.

In the course of a normal work day, you may have attended meetings, fielded customer service calls, spoken with co-workers, watched the news or witnessed a real-life event unfold. Make a mental note of the things you are exposed to and consider some of them as material for your blog

Get ideas from other writers

Read newspapers and magazines to learn what other people are writing and glean ideas from content that is already out there. If you like to blog about small business ideas, pick up a copy of Entrepreneur Magazine and read what experts in the industry are already writing about.

Formulate your own opinion about the subject and write away! (NOTE: Do not copy their article with only a few minor changes and make sure if you use any material from the original article you give full attribution to the source).

Research content aggregators

A great way to find good content is to browse websites like Technorati, Delicious and Stumble Upon. Content is continuously being fed into sites like these and they include a plethora of highly targeted subject matter for fresh blog ideas.

Use LinkedIn Groups

Another great online resource for ideas is LinkedIn Groups. Thousands of thought leaders introduce minions to great content through highly interactive group dialogue and can be a great source of ideas.

Make sure to browse through the group responses as many offer additional value that might not have been considered by the source of the discussion topic.

Create online "Alerts"

Both Google and Yahoo offer free alerts targeted to specific keyword phrases you consider important. Setting up alerts funnels relevant ideas to your email inbox that the search engines have picked up while indexing the web. These alerts can serve as a trigger for timely content and, like #1, help to create ideas to write about.

Conduct interviews

Find subject matter experts in your field of interest and ask them to do a short interview. People are looking for ways to generate low cost publicity and most are totally willing to share their views with you on your blog.

Invite others to blog

A new trend in generating blog content is to invite guests to blog on your site. Whether it's other experts in your chosen field or regular readers of your blog, asking for blog content is a great way to add more content, create "link juice" and help drive more people to read your blog.

If you do ask someone to Guest Blog, since they are getting free exposure on your site, make sure to ask for a return favor by having them link to your blog from theirs.

Develop a list

Creating a Top 10 list for things that relate to your niche is an excellent way to create content ideas and drive more interactions on your blog. If you blog about dogs, create a top 10 list of the best dogs for seniors. Invite comments to your blog and ask people to share their own feelings about your list.

Write tips on how to do something better

Do you have a special way of preparing salsa for party appetizers? Share your "secret sauce" with your readers.

One of the most important things you can do with your blog is to give the reader something of value.. a take-away that helps them to remember you and, more importantly, not feel as though they have been marketed to.

Create a post on your top posts

Kind of like "the year in review", summarizing your best blog posts for a specific period of time (or subject matter) offers readers the opportunity to consider and connect with multiple posts in one article. Make sure to link to your individual top 10 posts within the new summary article.

The bottom line is you don't always have to come up with revolutionary ideas to generate great content. There are tremendous opportunities that already exist to aid in creating great new content ideas for your blog. All you have to do is observe what is already being generated and develop your own perspective to share with others.

While it may be common for people to get overwhelmed with getting starting with a blog, there is no reason to feel like they are the only ones that don't know how to do it. Even people that have a few blogs up and running can easily get into a rut. That is very common too!

These common problems of getting started and getting stuck in a rut often cause some people to give up on blogging. I definitely struggled in these areas for a long time. I looked over programs that would eliminate these problem for me and help me get a clear direction on choosing blog ideas.

There is a system that is easy to follow and, yet, is not a get rich quick scheme. The best thing to look for when you are looking for a good system is finding someone that is making money and is willing to share their knowledge with you. You can pay anywhere from $199-thousands of dollars for this help.

Many times people make money with blogs but don't give you enough information to be successful yourself, or they want to charge you so much for their "valuable" advice. You can find a step-by-step program that literally covers everything someone would need to know about how to create and maintain a successful blog.

CHAPTER 3

STEP 2 - CHECK-OUT YOUR COMPETITION

Another important factor for how to start a blog is to take a look at your competition to determine what they might be doing. This is good market research! Spend some time on their blogs...

Hey, you've followed all the rules of SEO (more on that later), analyzed your keywords, optimized your blog and aligned your blog with your top competitor. You're doing the same things your competition is doing, you think. Now what?

You realize that the absolutely fabulous blog you've created needs something special. It must be able to stick out from a sea of millions of blogs all shouting for the attention of all those blog readers. Your content is relevant, yet your blog visitors are minimal. What do you do?

Well, you could spend your hard earned cash on a blog consultant. That might be pretty expensive -- just to diagnose your blog marketing problems. This could save you some time, but you would still have to implement those changes. Or, you could just follow these tips that I use daily to help you.

So, instead of paying out a bunch of money, here's a checklist that you can use to optimize your blog while increasing the amount of visitors you get.

1. Customize the look and feel of your blog using any number of free templates. Blogger is a good choice to start because it is free and easy to use even for a beginner. WordPress and Moveable Type are also very good, and they're also free.

2. Research your keywords and maintain a list of highly targeted keywords for your blog. They'll come in handy.

3. Activate automatic trackback and ping functionality on your blog. Check the settings of your blog, you should be able to just check yes or no to activate these things.

4. Utilize RSS Subscriptions, social bookmarking and tags or labels.

5. Create a Feedburner account so you can track your feeds and find out who is subscribing to your blog.

6. Find likeminded, authoritative blogs like ProBlogger, and link to them. Inbound links, the kind that link back to your blog, increase your search engine ranking and give you more credibility.

7. Remember to archive your posts for your readers' future reference. A reader may bookmark your blog because you had something relevant to share.

8. Request feedback or reviews of your blog in forums. Especially if one of your posts has relevance to a question or problem posed there.

9. Research and read relevant blogs and comment on them. This is a great way to build links as well as to develop professional relationships.

10. Post regularly, 3-5 times a week. I post daily, Monday through Friday for consistency sake.

These are just a few practical blog marketing and optimization tips to increase blog visitors as well as blog income. Doing these tactics every week will make your blog stand out from the rest.

The Importance of Branding

As a blogger the need for branding is huge. You cannot achieve the desired marketing growth if your lack proper marketing communication. A blog will do just that, it will communicate and help your online marketing. But how do you brand?

1. Segment the market

This way you will be able to identify your primary target and develop benefits that will appeal to them. With a segment for your product or your blog, you will be able to specifically target your offering; you will be having a clear picture of who your intended customers are.

2. Know your target

Understanding why they are buying from you is a big move that will help you in tailoring your products and designing your blog. Understand what sort of people they are, know their nitty gritty. This can be achieved by using subscription to be able to talk to them as often as you could make it personal.

3. Differentiate

This will make your offer unique. You will be different from your competition. Differentiate the way you sell your products, how you treat your customers. Have consistency in messages fonts, colour schemes. Get professional advice if you must but do it.

Your competitors will crush you if they get the chance, know them, and understand their plans, their customers, and their offer. Track, monitor their every move, anticipate their moves, it's a chess game, don't let the checkmate you.

Look at what is working and retain, throw away what is not working, innovate, turn your brand younger by the years, extend your brand, give your customers new experiences and change the rules of the game. It's the only way out.

4. Community

Be a hero on a speficic niche and create a trust, solid community around it. People by nature want to be part of something larger than them. People need a hero. They hero worship anything bigger than them. Niche marketing is your best shot. It creates niches which eventually turn into small tribes. Tribal brands are worshipped by clique of people and guarded secretly.

5. Build trust and consistency

A good brand is consistent, gives clear messages to its customer. Provides details of its benefits. Its benefits include both the extrinsic and intrinsic of the brand. It caters for its customers both functionally and emotionally. A good brand keeps its promise.

Consistency should be all round. The product quality should be the same. A bottle of coke is the same whether in a store in Atlanta or hawker cart in Tajikistan. Quality of a brand is in the color scheme, the way the name is written. Consistency is part of the promise. Part of the offer. It reassures your customer of lifetime relationship.

Since you know your customers very well, then you know what they want, why they want it, and you will always be able to remain relevant. While your competitors are stuck in old ways, you become distinct, standing out. Have easy tags, lines that even kids can recall. Live memorably to live longer.

Offer more than your competitors. This is the golden rule in marketing. Yes, with all the above then you will be offering more than your competitors.

CHAPTER 4

STEP 3 - BRAINSTORM SOME DOMAIN NAME IDEAS

Choosing a domain name for your blog is not an action to be taken lightly. Why is choosing a domain name such a big deal? Because, just like first impressions, you only have a few seconds before your audience decides to pay attention or move on to something else.

In most cases, your domain name is the first thing that your visitor will read. It must catch their attention and give them a reason to visit your website; otherwise your visitor will click to another page, and probably never come back.

In this chapter, we will discuss the major reasons and factors that should be taken when choosing a good domain name.

The main reason why a good domain name is important is because of search engine optimization. Choosing the right domain name has great relevance in search engines. A domain name can help improve ranking in keyword searches.

Many people often downplay the importance of a good domain name, however it is extremely important and must not be taken lightly. A good domain name should be keyword rich and can help you in your ranking position in searches.

How to Choose a Good Domain Name?

How do I choose a good domain name? I like to go to nameboy.com to find suggestion on the topic to find ideas for possible names. When searching for a domain name choose the ".com" extension especially if your target audience is in the United States, otherwise use the extension that is most popular for your audience.

The average cost for a ".com" domain name is about $10 a year. However, other extension can be a lot cheaper. From a visitors point of view a ".com" extension will be taken more seriously and have more credibility. I strongly suggest that you use ".com" if you are serious about your business. It is also the most common and widely accepted extension in the world.

Your domain name should be relevant to your content and should reflect exactly what you do. It should give your audience a crystal clear picture of what you are offering on your blog. Your domain name represents your brand or product. Each blog post and everything about your blog should be directly related to your domain name.

Here some basic rules in finding a good name:

<u>Your name must be describable</u>

It is very important that your blog's name have to describe your specific aim and niche or niches with your blog. The reason for this is that readers are going to search for a specific topic and if your blog's name is the same, they will end up at your site. They will also remember your blog's name and automatically the content of your blog.

Choose a name easy to remember

Let us say your blog is about gardening and home cleaning ideas. If you name it "The Blog with best gardening and home cleaning ideas ", it is definitely descriptive but I am not so sure if your readers are going to remember the name. Choose short and simple names like:

"Garden and Home ". This is also descriptive but easier to remember.

Try to choose a name similar to your domain name

This is a difficult one. To find a domain name in your specific niche is not so easy. In many of the cases that specific name is not available. I personally like the domain name ending on something.com, something.net or something.org.

If I have to choose, I will definitely go for something.com. However, if you believe that your domain name is perfect and it is not available on .com, then try with .net or .org, which are usually less busy. Otherwise, choose something similar and repeat.

If you cannot find your specific niche name for a domain, this is not the end of the world. You can use your own name as domain.

You can for example name it johnsmit.com. Brand yourself and your name on your blog and your audience will associate it with your specific niche. Your niche will then become a sub domain: e.g. johnsmit.com/gardenandhome/

Selecting the best name for your blog

Names are important, especially in the blogosphere. Having a memorable name can go a long way toward generating traffic for your site.

Choosing the right name can seem daunting, but these tips should help you in the process. Get a notebook, pen, a good place to work, and follow the steps below.

Begin your blog naming process by answering these 4 questions:

1) <u>Does your blog have a specific theme?</u>

For example, you may be hoping to blog about being a parent. Startup Daddy is a blog that was developed by a man who stays home with the kids and uses his blog to talk about being a parent and share his knowledge about small businesses.

2) <u>Who is your target audience?</u>

Make a list of different types of people you hope to reach. If your blog is about building amazing creations from Lego's, then think about places where you'll likely find your target market.

Lego forums? Legoland? The Brothers Brick blog picked a good name that should appeal to their target audience.

3) <u>Will you be blogging for hobby or for dollars?</u>

How you name your site can have a big impact on traffic and that's important if you're planning to be blogging for dollars someday. In this case, using the right keywords can come in handy. Start researching the most searched terms in Google and go deep from there, evaluating which is the best option to adopt for your name. That would increase the likelihood that your blog shows up when someone is searching the term on Google.

4) <u>What are some of the main blogs out there addressing this topic or targeted to this audience?</u>

You can do a search by going to your favorite search engine and type "blog search". You'll have several to choose from. Type in the them you're considering and see what blogs are listed.

Or you could consider the names of other blogs you like. Are the titles playful and fun, like the blog White on Rice Couple? Or do they communicate a theme like the Pioneer Woman?

Use this to take inspiration and to understand what type of blog you would love to have, so try to image yourself writing every day in the blog and figure out what would be the best style for it.

Now for the process of selecting that name.

1. Start Your Engines

Now that you've answered the questions above, it's time to get the creative juices flowing by doing some brainstorming. Do you know the rules for brainstorming? Me neither, but I know one thing: when you're brainstorming there are no "bad" ideas. Get your notebook and write ideas for your blog name.

Tell your internal critic to take a hike right now because you're all about quantity here; put down any words that come to mind. Oh, and tell your task master to take a hike too. (Yes, I often name and talk to the internal voices in my head. I recommend it!) If you start to think about the groceries you need, start a separate list to get that off your mind.

2. Free Association

Focus on some of the words you've written down in your brainstorming list and begin to build on those.

If your blog is going to be focused on how to be a master gardener (if so, please send me a link to your blog....I need help), you might have written the word "garden" on the list above. That's a great place to start. Now you can focus on that word for a while.

You might come up with additional words like: green, flowers, caterpillars, sun, growth, rose, green thumb, etc. Then you can pick a word from that list and focus on it for a while too. You can include concepts, songs, movies, and food, and more. The sky is the limit here! Hmmm, sky would be another good word for this list...you get the idea.

And the Winner is? Go back over your free association notes and circle words that strike you as interesting. Maybe from the words written above you like green, caterpillars, sky and growth. This is a great start!

3. Paring Down

Create a list of your top 20 blog name ideas. Maybe it's Green Sky, Caterpillar Keys, or Green Caterpillars.

4. Building Your Domain

Initiate a search of domain names. There are sites that can help you search a domain name to determine its availability and cost for purchase. If your goal is to have lots of traffic, experts on search engine optimization (SEO) recommend having a .com domain address free of punctuation if possible.

So if you liked the domain name "greencaterpillar.com" and you looked it up, you would discover that the domain name is available (at least it was when I checked). Excellent!

But before you send out a press release, notice that it's listed as a premium domain name. It's going to cost you nearly $1,000 to purchase it. Or you could purchase "greencaterpillar.info" for less than $1, but that might cost you in building traffic. Another option is to check websites like GoDaddy.com or WordPress and register for a domain name. You will pay a standard yearly commission, but it gives you immediate access to the domain and is much cheaper and faster. It is a good way to start, and buy the domain later on. The downside is the limited interface and personalization of the website, which is maybe not enough for a more advanced blog.

You'll need to decide how important having a .com address is for your site and the type of domain registration you want.

5. <u>Graphically Speaking</u>

Remember when selecting your domain name that you'll want to have a logo or some kind of graphic representation as your header for the site. Of the names you're considering, is there one that inspires a picture as well? You know what they say, a picture paints a thousand words!

6. <u>Get Feedback</u>

Talk to others about ideas for your blog name. Do you have particularly creative friends? Other bloggers? They would be great people to ask. You can also talk to friends, colleagues, relatives, or others who will give you trusted, honest feedback.

You might find out through one of your friends that green caterpillar is actually code for some illegal drug (in which case, do not ask why they know this information...). You want to consider the kind of traffic that a domain name like that could draw to your site.

7. Enjoy it!

It can seem a little overwhelming finding the right name, but you'll thank yourself in the end for taking the time to pick out the best name for your site!

Sit down with a notebook when you're learning how to start a blog and start jotting down a variety of names which get at the intent of your main topic idea and/or your spin. This will give you and your business a head start determining a terrific domain URL and providing you with the most flexibility and traffic at the beginning for your business blog.

To summarize, let it become a fun process. There are many affiliate marketers who are successful by selecting their own name, blog name and brand. Then there are those who make use of a special subject or use their experiences of the past to come up with a good name for their blog. You can also enjoy the process by playing around with words.

All of these techniques should help you achieve a perfect name for your blog site. I am sure that you can come up with great names if you follow the instructions well. Remember that choosing your perfect name will also benefit your branding in the future and avoid changes of name which will negatively impact your business. Therefore, I encourage you to take your time now to pick the right name, and be sure on your choice. Best of luck!

CHAPTER 5

STEP 4 - DECIDE ON A SOFTWARE/HOSTING

When you are learning how to start a blog, one of the major decisions you'll make is deciding on blogging software and hosting sites, make sure you are comparing apples to apples (and not oranges).

Many sites which claim to be "free" are anything but free. There are some perceived cheap options in the hosting world (or so it seems when you're just getting started!)

However, these options may cost you more in the long run since they do not actually provide you with a business building system (BBS) and the support you need and deserve to make your life easier and to help grow your business.

As you compare options, make sure you consider both your short-term and long-term needs for your business blog. Ask yourself what tools will be important to your business blog over time.

You'll want to read the fine-print and check out any site restrictions to determine if they will work or may negatively impact your future business plans.

Does your host offer you training (you'll need it for whatever type of business and software you're using)?

26

Look for a system that includes everything you need to build a business -- this includes built-ins which offer keyword searches, software built-ins so everything works together, e-zines, quality monetization models, constant upgrades as the internet and Google become smarter, and support forums to help you grow your business.

Beware of hosting systems requiring you to pay extra for every little plug-in you'll need to build a successful business.

With this type of hosting model, you're charged for each individual piece of business software including a separate fee for your domain name, domain hosting, blogging software, keyword searches plug-in, new business plug-ins, premium templates, e-zine support, traffic analytics, even extra charges for additional traffic as your blog followers grow, etc. This can cost your business a fortune!

Choosing the right blog software is a very important first step. You can compare it to needing to find the perfect vehicle. Sure, they will all get you from one place to another, but some are better at it than others. Some are quicker, more comfortable, and can be counted on to get you there.

The first thing you should ask yourself before deciding what is the best blog software is:

- Are you going to be a casual blogger that likes everything done for them?

- Or are you a more serious blogger who would like to make money and have the ability to customize your blog?

There are benefits and drawbacks to both "free hosting blogging services" and "blogging software" that you host on your own.

a) **Free hosting blogging services**

- WordPress.com
- Blogger
- Blogsmith
- Typepad

Benefits

- The service provides easy to use, point and click formats and templates that are "ready-made";
- The blogging service has a large staff behind it, thus you can go to them for technical assistance;
- No cost to host your blog (free hosting);
- Have a name brand behind them, thus give your blog posts a little clout in the search engines.

b) **Blogging software (host on your own)**

- WordPress.org (*different from WordPress.com, free blog service*)
- Expression Engine
- Textpattern
- Moveable Type

Benefits

- Huge flexibility and customization options with plugins and templates (as you'll see, it can require a tiny bit more work, but it's still simple and the upside is huge);
- Ability to make your blog look like a static website;
- Since you are hosting on your own server, you have full control of your blog. It won't get pulled down for various reasons (i.e. frowned upon marketing tactics).

In my opinion, and in the opinion of most web experts, WordPress.org, (the one that let you host on your own) is easily the best blog software and is head and shoulders above the rest in terms of quality, ease of use and flexibility.

Plus, it allows you to not be tied to the blogging format. You can use WordPress to create impressive websites as well. Using templates, you can literally have a gorgeous blog/website up in an hour. Moreover, utilizing the potential of their free plugins, you can seriously turn your WordPress site into a internet powerhouse!

Nonetheless, deciding which software to use to a large extent depends on your own particular plans. It's worth at the beginning having a fairly clear plan a tow here you would like to go. This matters because switching blog software mid-stream can be tricky, although in theory its easily doable between most platforms, but it's easier to stick with one if you can.

Think around things like do you want your own domain name, do you want to run advertising on it, and if so what sort of advertising. Do you want to be able to have really fancy templates or are you happy with a a really simple one. All these things will make a difference to what software you use.

Now, a common question is: how do you select the best blogging software?

There are many ways to generate income online. One of these is through blogging. This is why there are a lot of bloggers popping up. However, only a few of them are doing it right. Most bloggers keep on posting and posting but still end up generating only a few dollars every month.

Why is this so? What do successful bloggers have that their counterparts don't?

Surely not writing skills.

There are a lot of successful bloggers out there who know little about writing. But what they do know how to do is optimize and market. Optimization is the secret to being successful as a blogger... that and using the right blog software.

But with all the software that is available, how will you know which is the best? In the next chapter we are going to analyze and compare the most popular blogging software. However, here are 3 good ways to know if your software is the best blog software for you.

1. <u>Easy to use... for you!</u>

Whether you are an expert or a beginner in blogging, you are going to need software that is straightforward and uncomplicated to use. You would not want to clutter up your mind with things that you don't really need to know.

2. <u>Tracking, publishing and design tools</u>

These are the tools that are used to let search engines know that you have added new updates to your blog. In business, use of these tools is of utmost importance.

Tracking tools will give you data on who is regularly visiting your site. This will aid you in determining how much traffic you are getting.

Check the tools used for designing such as templates, plugins and text editors, just to name a few. Ensure that these are compatible with the programs you are using.

3. <u>Tech support</u>

Using new software can sometimes lead to a few problems. So you have to make sure that you can rely on tech support to help you out in case problems arise.

I encourage you to check on internet the level of assistance as well as the velocity of delivering support that the tech support gives to its client. Figure out what is best for you, and if still in doubt, trust your guts!

CHAPTER 6

BEST BLOGGING SOFTWARE FOR EASY BLOG MANAGEMENT

If you plan on starting a new blog then you can't really do without premium blogging softwares that automate the whole blogging process.

Blogging software is a program that allows online users to easily create, design and manage blogs. With a good blogging software, you can easily create and design a professional looking blog.

Until a few years ago, you were required to have a deep understanding of any of the complicated programming languages before you could even think about starting a blog! Fortunately, times have changed. Don't you just love ever-evolving technology?

Now, a blogging software provides both beginners and advanced developers the essential tools they can use to publish content online, with little or no programming experience. This software offers users a great range of customizable options to ensure they build good looking websites to showcase their ideas and content.

The use of this software makes it possible for users not to worry about any line of code messing their site layout so they can focus more of their energy on producing quality content for their readers.

Blogging software is being used by millions of webmasters to easily manage their online presence. So if you are thinking of establishing a strong online presence then these below software is among the things you must consider using.

Top Blogging Software for Beginners

WordPress

This software has two platforms, WordPress.org and WordPress.com. These are the top rated blogging softwares and are widely used by most webmasters due to the powerful features each of them provides.

WordPress.org is powering over 60 million websites worldwide but you have to host your website with a third party before you can be able to use it, unlike WordPress.com.

WordPress.org has an intuitive user interface and it's very easy to use. You don't need to be a developer or programmer before you can get around on it. The software comes pre-installed in most web hosting providers. It has thousands of free themes and plugins which you can use to add extra features on your site.

WordPress.com on the other hand is free blogging software and it doesn't require any third-party hosting. It's suitable for both individual webmasters and professional publishers.

Most beginners who are eager to establish online presence mostly start with this one because it is free and easy to use. It allows you to create a blog and start publishing blog posts within a few minutes. It's a powerful SEO friendly software that doesn't require much technical skills to get started. This software is also fully customizable and you can tweak it to get the kind of website you want.

Blogger

This is Google's own blogging software designed for individual bloggers, authors, and beginner publishers. It requires the users to only sign up with their Google account details. It's completely free to use and easy to setup. You don't need to have any programming skill before you can use it. Blogger has an easy-to-use drag and drop interface.

You can also use it to easily make money online because it's hard wired with Google AdSense and analytics. One of the big disadvantages of this software is that you would not be able to sell the website or blog you built on it if you ever decide to do so.

Tumblr

Tumblr is one of the most popular blogging software used mostly by beginners. The software is powering over 220 million blogs and over 100 Billion blog posts. It was owned by David Karp but was recently sold to Google to the tune of $1.1 Billion.

It is very easy to use with so many plugins and themes you can install to make your site look professional.

This software is more of a micro-blogging best suitable for people who are not looking for a long-term commitment into the world of the blogosphere. It allows users to sign up freely and start blogging.

Squarespace

Squarespace is standard blogging software that allows users to easily create professional blog and ecommerce Websites. You can use it to build an online store, showcase your products and services in a grand style. The first year annual plan comes with a free domain name. The software has millions of stunning images, customized email address, beautiful logo and much more.

Quora

Quora is a popular question and answer website used by professional and knowledgeable writers who already established with some amount of authority and expertise in their respective niche. If you plan on using Quora, just know that it doesn't allow customization. It's good for professionals who want to expose their brands to a huge number of online users. It's not the best blogging software for personal blogging.

Medium

Medium is a blogging software best suitable for those who want to be sharing stories and ideas. It's a pure social journalism platform and it doesn't offer users many customizable options. It's much like What-You-See-Is-What-You-Get with a wonderful web-based editor.

It's mostly used by individual bloggers who want to get their post read by as many people as possible. It has no widgets or plugins to move things around so you are pretty much on your own. The medium has nice clean and minimalist interface with a great social community.

MovableType.com

MovableType is a Content Management System for bloggers who want to build a good looking website. It makes publishing and managing of online business very easy, owing to the powerful features it provides.

MovableType has great many plugins and template editors that you can use to customize the look and feel of your Website/Blog. It's written in PerI, a popular scripting language that runs on almost every operating system which uses a variety of database to store blog content.

TypePad.com

TypePad is a paid blogging software but you can use it for free for a 14-day trial period. It's very easy to use in blog promotion and making money online. TypePad has great features that will skyrocket your blog to a great height. It has a text editor and HTML editor you can use to easily write and publish articles.

TypePad also comes with a great statistic tracking tool which includes average views per day, total page views, and bounce rate. It allows full customization of Templates for users that are on the unlimited package. It also has a good number of templates and you can use it to create several blogs.

CHAPTER 7

STEP 5 - CREATE GOOD QUALITY CONTENT FOR YOUR VISITORS

This is very important step when you are starting a blog! You want to provide your readers with good quality information - and you'll want to have a minimum of 30 pages, but 50+ is much better to get started with. Each of your pages should be between 350 - 500+ words (<350 are not enough to provide valuable information to your readers).

If you plan to make your blog a business, you will need to write proficiently for several hours each day... That's why it's so important to LOVE your topics and write about what you know and are interested in. Many bloggers will quit because this is work and it's a business! This requires dedication just like starting any other business.

When we're talking about how to start a blog, we'd be remiss if we didn't discuss the need for good quality original content. Your content needs to be interesting, honest, and you must be yourself when you're writing.

This means you can be witty, charming, motivating, or rugged depending upon your personality. Just keep it real! This will keep your readers engaged, interested, and coming back for more of your terrific featured articles.

Blogging is a lucrative way to generate more leads and income for your network marketing business. One of the keys to creating a blog that works is to do with quality posts. Let's take a look at 7 tips on how to produce quality content for your blog.

1. Do the Research First

The key to providing quality content for your blog is in using accurate, newsy, well thought-out information to populate your posts. Depending on the theme of your blog, you might not need to do a lot of research but using third-party information might go a long way in adding interest and a feeling of authority for your blog.

2. Include a Variety of Content

Maintain a central theme but write about a variety of topics that are logical detours or supplements to your market niche. A great way to produce quality content for your blog is by adding infographics, videos, music, power point slides and links.

Remember that you can always link within your blog to keep people from getting distracted on other websites. Another advantage to linking people to your own content is that you can show them more of the resources you have to offer.

3. Keep it Short

Producing quality content for your blog does not necessarily translate into writing long, information packed posts.

Remember your audience and consider whether or not the topic requires a lot of fleshing out.

The shorter, more informative, more entertaining posts will keep readers on your site, encourage them to share your blog with other potential leads, and keep them interested. A good rule of thumb is to write posts that are between 400-800 words.

4. Write Compelling Headlines

Think about the kinds of headlines that grab your attention and pique your interest. Producing quality content for your blog includes using an eye-catching title for your blog post. Consider some of the things that you search.

Something a lot of bloggers are doing right now are creating lists- 7 Tips on How to Create Quality Content for Your Blog, for instance. It worked right? Don't be afraid to play with the headlines until you see something that really commands attention.

5. Poll Your Readers

Ask them what topics they'd like to read more about. Getting readers involved can feel like a risk. What if they don't respond? It's a win-win either way. If your readers respond, you know they care and are reading what you write. If they don't, you already know your content needs to improve.

6. Keep a List of Possible Blog Topics

Producing quality content for your blog is much easier if you have a list of possible topics to reference when writer's block congests your creativity. Use an excel spreadsheet or input notes into your phone (or notebook, if you're old school) so you're never left without something interesting to say.

7. Proof Read and Post Later

Quality content is not written and published within the span of 30 minutes unless you can type faster than you can think and you're a grammatical genius. Once you've written your post, step away for 15-30 minutes, come back to it, and then spend a few intentional minutes proofreading your post.

And don't publish your post right away. Statistically, the best time to post is between 2pm and 6pm GMT Monday through Thursday. The simple reason is that people in America are getting their day started while people in Europe are winding down.

When you condense these 7 tips, it's really all about intentionality. Be intentional about your blog topic, be intentional in the sources and resources you use to tell the story, and then be intentional about proofing and posting. Incorporate these tips and you'll have lots of quality content for your blog.

Your blog should be the cornerstone of your marketing efforts. It's the place you drive traffic to, the forum that demonstrates your value and credibility. And if you incorporate an effective keyword strategy you can promote your blog posts and get them ranked on Google, as I have. Then your leads will flow like wine.

If you want to generate leads from the best prospects, a blog will help you do it. Read how to generate MLM leads with a blog here.

Write your blog content for folks with a short attention span - this is not a novel where folks will stick around until the end of the plot. They will be looking to gain their information in quick short bursts.

Creating content for your blog or site is an essential part of your market strategy. Creating Content is important, but marketing that content will make sure it gets bought. Creating content is extraordinarily easy, saves time and costs, reduces errors, ensures branding and compliance and improves customer service.

Creating content is probably the most important step to generating the best results for a company website. Creating content is a vital area of blogging that every blogger have to do regardless of topic, his style or whether he likes it or not (if you don't like it, why would you even start a blog.

Articles are one of the easiest ways to promote your website in order to generate traffic and increase your earnings. Articles are one of the most important factors in getting good search engine ranking. Writing articles is the best way to generate lots of traffic and sales online -without paying for it. Writing articles is the fastest, and most effective way to build an online business; with real foundations.

Writing articles is more than just putting pen to paper (or fingers to keyboard), but of promoting your online work of your home business both to search engine spiders, real people that want to learn more and will visit your website, blog or Squidoo lens to find what they want to learn. Writing articles is important when you are in business.

For example, let's say you're providing information on training dogs. Your article title would read something like: The Five Best Ways To Train Your Dog.

Or if you specialize in training German Shepard's, The Five Best Ways To Train German Shepard's. Your titles are the most important part of the article. This is where people who have German Shepard's want to know how to train them.

In your first paragraph, start off with your title, The five best ways to train your German Shepard is: Then proceed with sentence. Add the keyword German Shepard in every paragraph, this is going to assure relevance to what your audience is looking for while indexing you at the top of goggle.

At the end of your article one should always include: For more information about Training German Shepard's, visit Your website. Notice that I have added the keyword German Shepard's again.

These are very important steps to writing quality articles. Posting photos will also cut out the pics please emails and help sell you item quickly and easily. Posting photos will help you sell it, help your buyer find it, and probably give a number of others some new ideas when they see the photos.

Posting photos can be tricky at times, but it can be done if you keep a few things in mind during the process. Posting photos can allow you to help potential buyers and consumers as well as local business owners.

Posting articles can give incentives to users, but posting too many articles are not very productive. Posting articles can be a beneficial persuasive technique, but there needs to be an argument that this evidence supports.

Content is king when it comes to the internet and websites. Content however is not aimed at any particular age group, but may be enjoyed by all. Content is generated every time a connection is made between a buyer and a seller, or a perceiver and a receiver. Content can be easy to update and maintain even after the project has been distributed.

CHAPTER 8

STEP 6 - HOW TO START A BLOG & PROMOTE IT

One of the best ways to promote your blog is to gain traffic organically through the use of specific keywords being searched for by your visitors.

When you use the right keywords, the search engines will reward you by delivering your blog site to readers throughout the world. Get comfortable identifying specific words being searched within your niche.

Blogging Increases Your Market Share.

Unless you simply Blog for interest or for fun, I am guessing that you might just be interested in earning some money with your blog. Internet marketing and Blogging is a great mix with which you can do this, but first you need to understand how you can get your Blog noticed. So here are a few pointers as to how you can do this quickly and efficiently:

Your e-mail signature.

Every time you send an email, no matter what it is about, make sure you include a link to your Blog in your email signature. Most email systems will allow you to set this up quite easily, and this is a great way to have your blog noticed.

Understand Your Readers and Subscribers.

There are Blogging tools available which will allow you conduct regular surveys on your blog for your readers, in order for you to gain a better understanding of their needs and wants. This will then give you the information you need to provide this within your regular postings.

Ask for feedback on a post, ad links, or a product you have used. Again there are tools you can use to do this depending on which platform you choose to blog with.

Join a Blog Network.

By joining a Blog network, that is a network of blogs all sharing the same subject matter, and regularly posting comments, you will not only get your blog noticed, but will also gain some highly relevant back links which you need for the search engines to rank your blog highly.

The authority this gives is paramount to the authority which is then assumed by the likes of Google and Yahoo.

You will find as well that your readers and subscribers will assume your credibility is

good when they can link you to other blogs and information about your particular niche. In the internet marketing world the more bloggers the better.

Use an RSS Feed.

RSS is probably one of the fastest growing technologies on the Internet today. As such, having an RSS feed to your blog is of major importance, as it allows your readers and subscribers to be updated automatically whenever you add new content. Again, most blogging platforms will provide you with simple instructions or plug-ins to allow you to easily do this.

Don't Forget Social Media.

Blogging is part of Web 2.0 Technology, which means you can integrate with Social Media almost seamlessly. So adding Social share buttons to your Blog is also something which you must do if you want your readers to share your content easily. So Facebook, Twitter and YouTube (amongst the many others) can be utilized to the max.

There is simply nothing better than a Blog to provide you with the credibility you need to succeed online. In this day and age where advertising saturates our lives, Blogging with real people talking about everyday experiences, is a welcome and natural way for you to get your information out there.

You can easily become the known authority in your niche and be looked on as the "go to" expert within your chosen field of knowledge and expertise. So give your business a boost by using the blogging technologies available to you as your most effective Internet marketing tool.

Make sure to tell your family and friends about your blog - ask them to visit and give you constructive feedback. Make any necessary changes you think will help your blog.

Get your blog link published on your social media websites to encourage your social friends to visit your blog. Look for other media opportunities to get the word out about your blog. You can also advertise in hard copy magazines, online websites, or share links with other bloggers to encourage their traffic to visit your blog.

CHAPTER 9

MONEYMAKING VENTURES WITH YOUR BLOG

One of the trends these days when it comes to online ventures is making money online. In fact, a lot of people are going online to make money at the comforts of their own home.

As many people are bringing their businesses online, the opportunities to find money online are also great and this is one thing that makes people flock to online opportunities.

If you have an online journal or blog, you can actually make money from it as well. Indeed, blogs these days have evolved from being an online journal to a moneymaking venture. If you want to learn how to make money with your blog, here are some of the few things that you might find useful.

1. AdSense - Pay per click banner ads

This is a free program that you join through Google. Once approved you will have the ability to place a small bit of HTML code on your blogs. This code generates small ads that are relevant to your blog's content. Every time a visitor clicks on one of these ads, you are paid a certain amount per click.

2. Newsletters

It is new yet very useful technique to keep your reader updated and having one more opportunity to earn money from your online business. In your e-newsletter the chances of selling the space available on it can earn you good money with less effort.

Usually, you just need to make a newsletter, put some very useful content on it and let your potential client know about its quality. The ad you will get from this technique will be dependent on the number of readers or recipients of it, so make sure you have the good number of readers to present before your client.

3. Become a Brand Ambassador

If you love a brand and want to be their brand ambassador, you can package sponsorship opportunities, like incorporating ads or links into your posts, reaching out to your community on behalf of a brand. Doing a special campaign on twitter using branded has tags. The possibilities are endless!.

4. Affiliate programs

We all like to make sure we're buying the best products money can buy - your readers are no different to this and are more likely to make a purchase if you've found them the best product for them.

Choose products and companies with good reputations and quality sales pages. There is nothing worse than giving a glowing review of a product only to send your reader to a page that looks cheap and nasty.

5. Videos

Maybe your ad space is fine enough, but you can brand a video like you would a sponsored post, curate great content that would be useful for your viewers as well as the brand.

6. Digital Downloads

You can see this type of money making method in use on websites that sell ebooks or other digital download products like: WordPress themes, premium design resources, textures, etc. This works great because its a more passive way to earn income from your blog.

Once you set the link up for people to pay & download, you never have to touch it again and it can make you money over & over again. To streamline the process of digital downloads, I'd recommend checking out e-junkie.

With millions of users and the ability to sell your products for as little as $5.00 per month, e-junkie is the perfect solution to have someone pay (to your PayPal account) and instantly download your files.

7. RSS Feeds

If you have a blog, you would also be having a feed for sure. You can Place PPC ads in your feeds like that from AdSense or can also sell flat rate advertising. If you have burned your feed through Feedburner, you can easily add your AdSense ads in it.

8. Sell your Services

Depending on the type of blog you run, you can offer consulting services. Setting this up is as easy as adding a new post category called "Consulting." This option isn't limited to just marketers and entreprenuers, however. If you are a web designer, you would offer design services, which would fall under the same category.

Your consulting page should include a contact form, email and phone number, along with your past work experience and what services you are offering.

9. Job Announcements

All the popular blogs are trying to leverage job boards to make some extra income, Guy Kawasaki, ReadWriteWeb, Problogger... you name it.

Needless to say that in order to create an active and profitable job board you need first to have a blog focused on a specific niche, and a decent amount traffic.

The advantage of this method is that it is passive. Once you have the structure in place, the job listings will come naturally, and you can charge anywhere from $10 up to $100 for each.

10. Sell Design Templates

Provide blog templates for platforms that you have experience with to develop a niche market for your web design services. There are dozens of blog platforms online, with Blogger, WordPress, Typead and Live Journal being some of the most popular blogging tools.

More traffic will come to your website if you can offer blog templates that are compatible with a variety of blogging platforms. However, you will still be able to develop a large following by specializing in one specific blogging platform. Providing a wide variety of layouts will make it easier to get repeat customers when selling blog templates on your website.

11. Leverage the power of Google. You may think of Google as just a search engine, but it is in fact a huge internet powerhouse that offers unparalleled earning opportunities online.

One popular method is the Google AdSense program. Just sign up with the service to use space on your blog to show ads posted to Google. The system automatically displays advertisements related to the topics you write about in your blog.

If you wrote a blog about your pets, for example, the ads displayed would be for pet related products and information. If one of your readers clicked on an ad, you earn a small amount. When you reach a specified amount, Google sends you a check.

12. Look for community support - Many blogs have donation buttons on them, and they can get the job done. You'd be amazed at the number of readers who are willing to help out to keep their favorite blog going. The most popular way to use donation buttons is through Paypal.

13. Open an online store -If your blog is popular enough that it has become its own brand, it may be time to offer some souvenirs. This is easily done thanks to cafe press. The selling price is up to you; you just need to pay them the base price of the products.

14. Advertising revenue

You can earn a lot of money from the paid ads. You can sign up with the leading ad-revenue sharing websites and make money as a published for the content.

Google AdSense, Chitika, Kontera etc. are the leading advertising sites that review the content and show relevant ads on the blog. You can also rent advertising spaces on the blog manually and generate handsome amount of money.

15. Flip your blog

If you're already making some money from your blog, you can flip the website for a handsome one-time amount.

This isn't a true passive income source, but a blogger who's eager to write on different topics can follow the method and make his living just by flipping the blogs. The concept is almost same like generating money from ad revenues; but in this method, you will earn a good one-time cash to invest in some other business.

If you love blogging, you can turn this hobby into a lifelong passive income generator. Explore all the methods how you can monetize the content and find the best blend to maximize your earning potentials.

Blogging has become a very popular method of making money online. Literally millions of bloggers are trying to make money from their blogs, writing on their favorite topics. The successful bloggers around the world also inspire the newbies and encourage them to write online and get royalties in a unique, modern way.

If you have developed a blog already, you can easily monetize the content and start making money almost instantly. But in case, you haven't prepared a blog or it doesn't have sufficient content, you have to concentrate on preparing the website and generate traffic to the blog to make money.

Once you have completed the homework that is built a blog and generated some traffic, you can follow any of these techniques or combine them suitably to earn money for the contents you have already published online.

CHAPTER 10

HOW TO ACHIEVE GOOD PERFORMANCE WITH YOUR BLOGGING

Sometimes getting to the point where you're receiving income from blogging just seems to take forever before you start to see the money flowing! Why is that?

Because that's the way is with everything. Poor performance equals pain and a bad life. Poor marriage partners end up divorced, poor parents find their kids in jail. Fair performance isn't much better in the results department.

Good performance usually equals fair results, sometimes you can get by, and sometimes you still lose your job with just "good performance". And that's where most of us stay.

So what kind of performance does it take to get income from blogging?

Achieving income from blogging with internet marketing requires to step up to the plate and commit for once and for all that you can do it and drive yourself. Excellence performance will equal leads to start flowing in.

And, don't stop there, because outstanding performance will equal HUGE benefits! And, there's really not much of a leap between excellence and outstanding performance in the form of how much work you have to do.

So the trick is to hang in there and be persistent with a technique that is beginning to allow you success, and build on that beginning success to move yourself from excellent to outstanding performance.

Start learning about the right "income from blogging" strategy to become outstanding...

You need to understand what makes blogs rank. Just blogging willy-nilly with no rhyme or reason strategy could get you nowhere. The first thing to consider when looking to acquire income from blogging is your keyword phrase.

The title in your blog post should include the keyword phrase you're blogging about. This should also put it in the "permalink" which is that Google looks for when ranking. Make sure that your keyword phrase is in your title, your first sentence, last sentence, and in three different subheadings in your blog post.

Lots of backlinks to your blog post will generate ranking, which generates income from blogging...

You want as many people as possible to read and comment on your blog post, so remind your reader to comment. When other people like your material and link their own material to yours, a backlink is created. You can also create your own backlinks by linking online articles or YouTube videos you create to your blog post.

Use a high authority blogging site to link to for generating income from blogging

While the above strategies for backlinks will work, I also strongly advise you link to a high authority blogging site to get the SEO juice flowing. It's a great idea to be a part of a team blogging system, as a team blog will be much more popular on Google and any individual blog site.

Google ranks according to relativity and popularity. Your keyword phase will make it relevant, and linking to a team blog site or using a team blog site to blog from will give you automatic popularity.

CHAPTER 11

MAJOR CHALLENGE IN BLOGGING

The major challenge that many blog owners (bloggers) are facing is inadequate targeted traffic. Without targeted traffic, a blog will never flourish. When you realize that your blog isn't attracting enough targeted traffic, you shouldn't give up.

It is normal for anyone to feel discouraged due to disappointments but giving up isn't a solution. Giving up is creating another problem of having not found a solution that works effectively. The best you can do instead of giving up is to find out how you'll drive targeted traffic to your blog.

So, why is your blog not receiving targeted traffic? Some of the reasons are as follows:

1.) Your blog is yet to be known since it is still new. It requires exposure.

2.) There is no enough content on your blog to attract people and for the search engines to rank your blog.

3.) The content you have published on your blog isn't of high-quality. Publishing mediocre content on your blog could be the reason why it lacks targeted traffic.

4.) The niche of your blog could be the reason for insufficient targeted traffic. If your blog is targeting a niche that is too competitive or the one that people are not interested in, then your blog will not attract any significant amount of targeted traffic.

5.) You haven't started selling a product that solves a particular problem or you could be selling a product that isn't useful.

6.) You haven't optimized your blog in the search engines. You have not used the search engine optimization techniques to optimize your blog.

7.) You haven't done list building and this has led you not to keep in touch with people who visit your blog. They visit your blog never to visit it again since they forget it.

8.) You have not captured people's attention. Your blog doesn't have content that is interesting for people to read. You haven't used headlines that will capture the attention of people. You haven't also posted videos or pictures that capture people's attention. You're not giving giveaways. People love getting things for free!

9.) Your blog contains many spelling and grammar mistakes. People will not want to go on reading a blog that has posts containing many spelling and grammar mistakes.

10.) Another reason for lack of targeted traffic is ignoring the readers and writing for the search engines. Focusing mainly to optimize your blog in the search engines instead of focusing on your readers will eventually make your readers to stop visiting your blog.

CHAPTER 12

WAYS OF INCREASING TRAFFIC

Driving targeted traffic to your blog is a process that should be continuous. Here are ten ways that you can use to drive targeted traffic to your blog.

1.) Update Your Blog Regularly: You should start updating your blog regularly with fresh content that is unique and informative if you haven't been doing that.

2.) Quality Content and Not Quantity Content: Although you should update your blog with fresh content, it doesn't mean that you should update it with any content for the sake of updating it regularly.

High-quality content is important in retaining your existing targeted traffic. Posting high-quality content will make people to visit your blog since they know that they're going to benefit a lot.

3.) Gain Exposure for Your Blog: Use internet marketing techniques that will ensure your blog gains exposure. Some of the internet marketing techniques that you can use include social networking sites, search engine optimization ways, viral marketing, pay per click Ads, Google AdWords etc.

4.) Keep in Touch with Your Audience: You have to do list building. Let the people who are visiting your blog to give you their email addresses willingly. You'll later on contact them so that you remind them to visit your blog.

5.) Attract People's Attention: Capture people's attention so that they can keep on visiting your blog. Use headlines that will capture people's attention to read your blog posts. You should also post videos, infographics and include pictures on your blog posts so that they attract people's attention.

6.) Avoid Spelling and Grammar Mistakes: Proofread your articles. Let someone else read your articles before you publish them on your blog. This is to ensure that your articles don't contain spelling and grammar mistakes.

7.) Engage Your Audience: You need to engage your audience. Ask them questions and let them comment on your blog posts. Reply their comments. This way, your audience will know that you appreciate them and value their opinions. Your audience will trust you and they'll keep on visiting your blog and also refer people to visit your blog.

8.) Allow Guest Blogging: You should invite experts to publish content on your blog. When you allow experts in your field of specialization to do guest blogging, your blog will gain good reputation. People will trust it and this makes your blog to be authoritative.

9.) Quality Products: Selling high-quality products will make people to visit your blog. A word of mouth will spread much faster about your blog if you're selling high-quality product that is solving a particular problem that other products haven't been able to resolve.

10.) Buy Traffic: Buying traffic will at least make people to know your blog. There are many websites that specialize in selling traffic.

CHAPTER 13

TIPS TO SUCCESSFUL BLOGGING

Blogs can be a very marketable and very profitable tool if used correctly. Profiting from blogs is just a matter of grabbing the attention of an audience and not doing any actual salesmen selling. In this article you will learn the 13 most essential steps to successful blogging.

1) Where to start?

You should begin your blog with a free blog hosting service such as Journal Home or Blogger. Starting with a free blog hosting service allows you to begin blogging instantly without having any advance knowledge of scripts, hosting, or programming. It allows you to focus on your content and not the internal maintenance of the blog.

The best benefit of starting with a free service is, in the case your blog doesn't become successful you do not lose any money or are you left holding the bill. The great thing about a blog is that they are organized in chronological order, your latest entry is displayed first.

When your blog traffic grows greatly and you are ready to upgrade to your own domain then you can simply make your last blog entry the announcement of your "move".

Simply add a last entry stating that your blog has "moved" and type the new blog URL address. Which directs visitors to your new blog site, keeping your following, without a major inconvenience to anyone. Upgrade as you need to...but only when you need to!

2) Niche

A niche is a targeted product, service, or topic. You should first decide on a product, service, or topic which interest you. Choose an area which you can enthusiastically write about on a daily basis.

You can use keyword research services like Google Zeitgeist or Yahoo! Buzz Index to find popular searched topics. It does NOT matter if your topic is popular as long as there is a audience for your topic and the topic is precisely focused then your blog should be successful.

Anything can be considered a niche as long as it has a target audience no matter how large or how small the audience is.

A blog about your cat can be a niche or a blog about the species of the cat family can be a larger niche market, if there are people who are interested in hearing about your cat or the species of the cat family...you can even choose to build your audience for a market which an audience does not exist, but first you must build your blog.

3) Update Daily (nothing less)

This step is a must and not a suggestion. Updating your blog daily not only keeps your blog more interesting to readers, but it also gives your blog fresh content on a day to day making it more appealing to search engines.

Not updating your blog on an occasional holiday or one day here and there is understandable to most, but missing days at a time or weeks is unacceptable and will most likely result in your blog being unsuccessful. To keep your blog traffic and retain your visitors interest it is a must to update your blog daily with multiple entries.

You should try to update your blog everyday with at least 3 or more daily entries. The best way to accomplish this is to set aside 1-2 hours a day for tending to your blog and adding new entries. It may even be wise to schedule a set time which you dedicate to your blog each day.

Give yourself work hours and treat your blog as a job, what happens if you don't come to work for days or weeks...you lose money or worse you get fired! Same applies here...if you don't update your blog for days or weeks you'll lose visitors.

4) Traffic

It's no secret. You must have traffic to profit from blogs. There are numerous ways to build traffic. Paid advertising, free advertising, viral marketing, search engine marketing, RSS/XML feeds, and word-of-mouth.

You should always use your blog URL address in the signature of your email, forum discussions, message boards, or any other communication media. You should submit your blog URL address to search engines and blog directories.

You should submit your RSS/XML URL feed to blog ping services like Technorati, Ping-O-Matic, and Blogdigger. You should confidently share your blog with family, friends, co-workers, associates, and business professionals when it relates.

Many blogs can be considered as a collection of articles, for this purpose you should submit your blog entries (those that are valuable and lengthy articles) to content syndicators like GoArticles.com or ArticleCity.com. Once submitted your articles can be picked up and published by others.

The trick is to make sure you include your Blog URL address in the "About the Author" passage.

What this does is create link popularity and backlinks for your blog, when someone picks up your article from the syndication then publish the article on their website the "About the Author" passage is included with each publication and the link you included is followed, crawled, and indexed by search engines.

Imagine if your article is popular enough or controversial enough to produce 10,000 publications across the web.

The search engines is bound to find your site in no time with that many publications and credit you a authority on the topic, in return increasing your rank on search engines.

The small effort of writing a well written article is rewarding. You should try to write at least 1 full length article every week for syndication and submit your article to at least 10 article syndicators.

5) Track Your Blog

How do you know if your blog has traffic? Just because no one is leaving comments doesn't mean your blog isn't growing. Many visitors do not leave comments but they are returning visitors.

I know it sounds crazy but with blogs people are more interested in what "you" have to say! Many visitors do not comment their 1st, 2nd, or 3rd time. Some do not comment at all, but are active daily visitors.

Tracking your blog does not have to be overly sophisticated usually a simple free page counter like StatCounter.com or Active Meter will do the trick. Install (copy/paste) the code into the html of your blog template and start tracking your visitors.

Its better to use a service which gives you advanced traffic analysis, such as keyword tracking information, referral information, and search engine information. Visitors, returning visitors, and unique visitors should be standard for any page counter service you choose.

6) Listen to Your Audience

When using the proper page counter you should begin to see how others are finding your blog and if through search engines then which keywords are being used to find your blog.

If constantly your blog is being found by 1 or more keywords then focus your blog around those keywords to make it even more powerful. When writing entry titles and entries use the keywords as often as possible while keeping the blog legible and interesting.

7) Multiple blogs

Use multiple blogging accounts to attract more people. This means you should have a blog with JournalHome.com, Blogger.com, LiveJournal.com, Blog-City.com, tBlogs.com, etc.

The more blog accounts the better. You can copy/paste from 1 blog to all others. Having different blog accounts is like having a publication in different newspapers. This enables you to attract more visitors and this also increases the chance that 1 of your blogs will be in the search engine results for your focused keywords.

8) Short & Concise

Aside from the lengthy article a week for syndication and publication your blog entries should be short & concise (if you can help it). Sometimes there are exceptions to the rule and you have no choice but to blog lengthy entries, but try to avoid this as much as possible. You do not want your blog entries to become hours of reading.

Visitors like to easily find information and skim through your entries. It is good to be detailed and provide useful information, but do not include useless information or run away sentences that veer away from your topic.

9) Digital Art

Try to include non-advertising graphics, pictures, photos, and art in your blog entries. Not too much. Once a week is fine. Graphics can sometimes bring your blog to life. Of course, the content of the blog is the most important aspect and you do not want to overshadow your content with graphics, but displaying graphics can add a bit of spice to the blog.

Be choosy about your graphics and make sure they fit your entry topic. You should add content with the graphic, at least a caption. Original graphics, photos, pictures, and art is recommended.

10) Keep it Personal

A blog is most successful when it is kept personal. Try to include personal experiences which relates to the topic of your blog entry. Stay away from the business style of writing.

Write with a more personal style and use first-person narratives. Do not write any of your entries as sales letters, instead share product reviews and personal endeavors.

11) Interact With Your Visitors

You now have the traffic you deserve. You should begin interacting with your visitors. Create a regular theme such as: "Monday Money Tip" or "Picture of the Week" which entices your readers to look forward to each week.

Give your readers advance notice about a product, service, or topic which you are going to review and then talk about later. If the President was scheduled to give a speech then in your blog you should state that you "will discuss the speech and give your opinion after the speech airs. Comments will be appreciated".

Try your best to find exclusive information that not many have. Do not disclose any confidential or secret information which is deemed illegal or can potentially get you into trouble, but try to get the scoop before everyone else does.

Such as: If your blog was about Paris Hilton (the socialite) and you had a blog entry about "Paris Hilton Getting Married" then it would be interesting to your readers if you had a actual picture of Paris Hilton engagement ring.

Give your best effort to dig and search the internet for exclusive information and you will possibly come up with something useful. Your readers will appreciate this and they show their appreciation through word-of-mouth referrals. Imagine how many readers will tell their friends, family, and others about information they only can find at your blog.

12) Make Money

Once your blog has gained some real momentum and your blog traffic is increasing then it is time to start thinking about turning your traffic into profit. You should use contextual advertising, like Google AdSense or Chitika.

Contextual advertising is usually text links which use the content of your blog to publish targeted ads on your blog. The payout is usually based on a pay-per-click model, meaning for ever click an ad receives you are paid a small percentage of the profits.

In addition to contextual advertising it is good to also use graphical advertising such as: BlogAds.com, Amazon.com, MammaMedia, or General Sponsored Advertising.

13) You're a Professional

You're a professional now! What are you still doing with that free blog hosting service? It is time to upgrade to a domain hosted solution. You need to get a web host and choose a domain name for your blog then check its availability.

Select the blogging software you wish to use, such as: Squarespace.com, WordPress.org, MovableType.org, etc. When you have your new blog domain setup and ready for traffic then it is time for you to announce your move on all your previous blog accounts. Your last entry to the blog should be a "move" announcement.

The title should be "Moved" and the blog entry should state something like "Old Blog has been moved to New Blog please follow and bookmark this link for future reference. This way all returning visitors and new readers should not have any problem finding your new blog domain.

At the level of a professional blogger you may want to team up with 1 or more other bloggers. This will create a more interesting and more powerful blog. The old saying "two heads is better than one", more authors mean more advertising and exposure because each author will have a vested interest in the blog.

The idea of a team blog is to make it profitable and rewarding for all authors, while continuing to target the blog topic and keeping the blog interesting for visitors.

Following these blogging techniques should make your blogging experience much more rewarding. There is no guarantee that your blog will become popular or a household name, but the effort should at least put you one step closer.

Making money online is not an overnight experience like many may think, but making money online is definitely a foreseeable possibility. As well, growing popularity on the web is not an overnight experience, but through time, dedication, and persistence you will be rewarded with all the royalties of blogging.

CONCLUSION

Every day many things occur around us. Some things are good, and some things are wrong. Blogging offers us an opportunity of sharing our thoughts regarding those things. In addition, it is a good way showing your creativity to the world.

You can write whatever you think, and blogs have a much better impact than social networking posts. You can encourage people for good things, show them a right way of doing something and raise your voice against something bad taking place in the world. Here are some impressive reasons why you should start a blog today.

It is true that many people search for the solutions of their problems. Some people want to know health tips, some search for better career options and some love to read about new technologies. You can address those readers through your blogs.

There are many attractive topics to choose from. Pick your favorite one and start writing. If your ideas are good and helpful, you will get many readers for your blog and thus you can help others. It is a way of helping others because your offered solutions and ideas can provide readers with better ideas and helpful solutions.

Practice makes man perfect; it is a renowned quote, and it is true. Probably you may think that you are not a good writer, but you should write. In starting you may get failed in tempting a large number of readers, but you will get some readers for sure.

You can improve your writing skills with regular blogging and become a great writer. You will get better ways of presenting your thoughts in the blogs and articles if you continue blogging. That's what many bloggers did and today they are succeeded in this field.

Some people think that blogging is easy and just a hobby, it is not true. Blogging is quite challenging, especially if you have never done it before. You need to think very deeply before you write for any topic. You also need to think about its impact on readers.

Today's world needs bloggers, who can help in making this world a better place to live. It is all about choosing words carefully and set them in the form of a blog to send a right message. You can take it as a challenge and challenges are good for life.

Blogging is not only done to help the readers for their needs but also done to earn good money. Probably, you may know that there are many writers and bloggers, who make hundreds of dollars weekly by their blogs. You can be one of them if you get a large number of readers.

It is quite easy to start a blog on any blogging platform and make it live. You can write on hot topics and let people read your blogs. It will fill your account with bucks, which will encourage you to write more on new things.

Nowadays hundreds of bloggers are sharing their thoughts online. Many of them write on same things in different ways. A well-promoted blog gets the larger number of readers in comparison to simple blogs.

You should check some SEO tips and online promotion ideas if you want to make your blog the main source of your earnings. There are websites, which provide latest techniques to promote a website or blog online. Get in touch with those websites and try your best to promote your blog.

Blogging brings many new things to the life with a good chance of making good money. Writing can become your hobby and a way of sharing your thoughts with others. Starting a blog is quite easy, but it takes an expert's mind to promote it and draw the attention of readers.

Online promotion can help you, but you should be active on social networking platform to gain more readers. Thus, you will get readers for your blog, and then you can sort out many issues of their life through your blogs. People love reading and blogs are free to visit and read. You can make it a source of expressing what you think and that will be valuable for your readers.

Thank you again for purchasing this book!

Made in the USA
Las Vegas, NV
12 December 2023

82643142R00049